The Boy Whose BUM Fell Off!

by

Geoffrey Herringshaw

This book is based on a TRUE STORY!

When Tommy came home for his dinner one day
he got an unusual surprise.

He suddenly found that he couldn't sit down
no matter how often he tried.

Yet when he looked down to investigate this
the problem was not with his chair.

But something else he often sat down upon
was oddly just no longer there!

The reason that Tommy just couldn't sit down
and couldn't tuck into his tea

was strangely because he was missing his bum!
Now, just where on earth could it be?!

As Tommy's dad looked at this he was confused.
'Now, that's most unusual,' he sighed.

'It's easy to lose quite a lot of your things
but strange to mislay your behind!'

'It must have dropped off as I played in the park,'
said Tommy, 'though I don't know where.'

'Well, let's go and check,' said his dad, 'but I hope
in future you take better care.

For last week you lost both your pen and your hat
a week or two after you got 'em.

And now you've come home and are telling me that
you seem to have misplaced your bottom!'

'We'd better go out to the park for a look,'
said Tommy's dad, 'that's what we'll do.'

'Okay,' Tommy said, 'but before we go out
can I quickly go for a poo?'

'I'm not sure you can,' Tommy's dad pointed out.
'You'll find it's not easily done.

For how do you think that you'll manage to poo
if you are now missing your bum?

As now that it's gone you may struggle to do
a lot of the things that you like.

Like taking a poo, sitting down for your tea
or having a ride on your bike!'

'I just hadn't thought about that,' Tommy said.
'We'll track it down if we're in luck.

Let's go out right now and just hope that we do
before someone else picks it up.'

But as they were making their way to the park
they saw a sign outside a pub

that made Tommy wonder if people like him
were meeting at some kind of club.

The sign that they saw said a 'bottomless brunch'
was taking place right at that time

and Tommy, not knowing what this really meant,
was keen that they both go inside.

'Well, just look at that!' Tommy said, 'it's a place
where people like me can all come

and meet up with others who, just like I did,
have ended up losing their bum!'

But Tommy's dad now had to break the bad news:
'I'm sorry, it's not what you think.

A bottomless brunch is a meal where you have
no limit on how much you drink.

So nothing to do with not having a bum,'
he said, which made Tommy dismayed.

'Well, that's quite misleading!' was Tommy's reply.
'A clearer sign should be displayed!'

So onwards they went and were soon at the park
and carefully looking around.

Then Tommy's dad saw Tommy's face had lit up.
He'd spotted his bum on the ground!

But right at that moment, as Tommy reached out
to pick up his bum from the floor

a dog then appeared and, to Tommy's surprise,
ran off with it clasped in its jaws!

So Tommy yelled 'quick!' and they started to run
but that didn't do any good.

The dog was quite clearly too quick for them both
and disappeared into a wood.

A few moments later the dog reappeared
and ran back to where it had been.

But Tommy saw nothing was gripped in its teeth.
His bum was nowhere to be seen!

But as they stood wondering what they should do
a boy ran by wearing a hat.

And Tommy's dad saw this, looked puzzled and said,
'there's something not right about that.'

Then as he looked closer he saw that this hat
was rather unusual and said,

'look, Tommy, that boy who just went running by,
was wearing your bum on his head!'

They thought they could probably catch the boy up
so once again started to run.

As now it seemed clear they were ever so near
to catching the runaway bum.

But as they began to catch up with the boy,
before they had managed to speak

a seagull swooped down from right out of the sky
and grabbed Tommy's bum in its beak!

They watched in dismay as the bird flew away
and carried the bum through the sky.

'I think that we've lost it,' observed Tommy's dad.
'I don't know what else we can try.'

'I'll just have to wait for my bum to grow back,'
said Tommy, 'what else can I do?

How long will it be 'til it's just like it was?
Will it take a month, or take two?'

'Your bum won't grow back like your hair,' said his dad.
'But doctors should know what to do

and I would think they will be able to make
a robotic bum just for you!'

'We might get your bum back one day,' he went on.
'Though maybe not anytime soon.

So maybe 'til then we could use something else,
like cushions or even balloons.'

'Yes, we could attempt to do that,' Tommy said.
'Perhaps for a while I'll pretend

a cushion, a beanbag or pair of balloons
is actually my rear end!

But hopefully that would be just for a while.
For now, to fill in, whilst it's gone,

as I'll keep on hoping I get my bum back.
I want my original one!'

'I know, but for now let's go home,' said his dad.
'It's starting to get a bit dark.

I'm sure the lost property office will help.
Your bum may get found in the park!

And so if it is and it gets handed in
we'll prove that it's yours and was lost

but now there's not really much more we can do
than go home with our fingers crossed!'

But as they were making their way through the park
they passed by a bench near a willow

on which slept a man who was resting his head
upon a most odd-looking pillow!

As Tommy looked closer his face soon lit up.
'Can you see what this man has done?

He's fallen asleep but he's made a mistake.
His pillow is really my bum!'

'You'd better just check that you're right,' said his dad,
'as that thing may not be your bottom.

For sometimes you see things and think that they're bums
but very soon realise they're not 'em!'

But as they got closer they couldn't deny
the man was asleep on a bum.

So Tommy's dad woke him and said, 'pardon me,
but that thing belongs to my son.'

'I know that it's comfortable,' Tommy went on,
'I've sat on it thousands of times.

But please let me show you the gap where it was
to prove that it used to be mine!'

The man rubbed his eyes as he pondered all this.
'I'm awfully sorry,' he said.

'It dropped from the sky as a seagull flew by,
and that's why it's part of my bed.

But now I can see it's undoubtedly yours
of course I'll return it to you.

I'll get off it now and, here, please have it back.
That's clearly the right thing to do.'

So Tommy was grateful his bum was returned
and put it right back in its place.

But after he'd done it he saw that the man
had quite a sad look on his face.

And Tommy's dad said, 'now you've nothing to use,
and nothing to cushion your head.

But if you wait here then I'll nip to the shop
and get something better instead!'

A few minutes later he'd made his way back
and carried a bag in his hand.

Then took out a comfy new pillow he'd bought
and handed it straight to the man!

The man thanked them both and then lay down again
before he went right back to sleep.

And Tommy, so grateful he'd got back his bum,
then let out a sigh of relief!

When Tommy's dad noticed the look of relief
that spread right across Tommy's face

he said, 'well, I hope that you've learnt how some things
can be rather hard to replace!

Whilst losing a pen or a toy or a hat
can all be quite easily done,

replacing those things is much easier than
locating a runaway bum!

Now, hopefully all that has happened today
has shown you the things you can't do

when missing your bum, such as riding a bike
or sitting and having a poo!'

'It has!' Tommy said, with a smile on his face,
'and from this day forward I swear

I'll never again lose my bum and make sure
I treat it with much better care!'

But Tommy now paused and looked thoughtful and said,
'Yes, I've learnt a valuable lesson!

But all of the things that have happened today
have made me ask one final question…

On everyone's body the head's at the top,
the feet are right down on the floor.

Yet what's called a 'bottom' is in between those,
so not at the 'bottom' at all!

So if you think carefully then you will see
that it's quite a puzzling riddle

We call it that name for that's not where it is…

We really should call it a 'middle'!'

The End

Printed in Great Britain
by Amazon